Hipp

A Text

for Students

with Introduction, Translation, Commentary and Notes

by
Geoffrey J. Cuming

GROVE BOOKS LIMITED
Bramcote   Nottingham   NG9 3DS

CONTENTS

PREFACE

It is now just on forty years since Dom Gregory Dix produced his edition of the *Apostolic Tradition* of Hippolytus. That edition remains indispensable to scholars as a work of reference, but it was never really suitable for beginners, who were bewildered by the very fullness of the textual apparatus and the complicated typography of the translation, with its four types of brackets. On the other hand, B. S. Easton's edition has been justly criticized for presenting an over-simplified picture of the evidence.

This edition tries to avoid both pitfalls. The variety of source-material is made plain, but only the bare minimum of variant readings has been included. No attempt has been made at a hypothetical reconstruction of the original; each section is translated as it stands from the oldest source, be it Greek, Latin, Coptic, or Ethiopic. Other versions are brought in only when they provide an obviously superior reading. In this way the beginner is given a clear impression of the situation without having to find his own way through a luxuriant jungle of footnotes.

The editor's indebtedness to the editions of Dix and Dom Bernard Botte will be immediately obvious; much help has also been derived from the two volumes by J. M. Hanssens, which are less well-known to students in this country.

In addition, acknowledgments are due to the Leverhulme Trust for a generous grant which made the research for this study possible, and to rhe Curators of the Bodleian Library for permission to use their photographs on the front cover. Part of the translation which follows has previously appeared in R. C. D. Jasper and G. J. Cuming *Prayers of the Eucharist* (Collins, 1975).

Geoffrey J. Cuming
September 1976

PUBLISHER'S NOTE

Since Geoffrey Cuming originally edited this Liturgical Study, he has added to it a companion volume, *Essays on Hippolytus* (Grove Liturgical Study No. 15, 1978), which is designed to go closely with the text in this one—but it is not cited here solely because the 1976 impression has been revised as little as possible. Similarly, there is now a Joint Liturgical Study no. 2 *The Canons of Hippolytus*, edited by Paul Bradshaw and Carol Bebawi, but not cited here.

First Edition December 1976
Reprinted August 1979
Reprinted February 1984
Second Edition (by Grove Books Limited) July 1987

ISSN 0306-0608
ISBN 1 85174 056 2

INTRODUCTION

Most liturgical texts have come down to us in the form of a few manuscripts differing in detail, but substantially and obviously containing one and the same work. With the *Apostolic Tradition* of Hippolytus, the case is very different; and before the text can be read with profit, its history must be set out in all its complexity.[1]

The Sources

In 1848 the manuscript was published of a previously unknown church order written in the Bohairic dialect of Coptic. It had no title nor any author's name, and subsequently became known as *The Egyptian Church Order*. Later in the nineteenth century, manuscripts of the same work were discovered in Sahidic Coptic, Arabic, Ethiopic, and finally, Latin. All these manuscripts contain collections of church orders whose contents do not completely correspond with one another. The Church Order was a literary form characteristic of the early centuries, a well-known example being the *Didache*. It would contain rules for Christian life and church discipline and liturgical forms, often attributed to the twelve apostles. From the fourth century onwards such Orders were often gathered into collections. Sometimes they were drastically re-written, or cast into the form of canons, and even those that were not re-written were liable to alteration to fit the customs of the time and place of writing. The anonymous Order, which for the moment we will call **X,** forms part of various collections which are tabulated below.

TITLE	*LANGUAGE*	*CONTENTS*
(Anonymous collection)	Latin	1. *Didascalia.* 2. *Apostolic Church Order.* 3. **X.**
Apostolic Constitutions **(AC)**	Greek	1-6. *Didascalia.* 7. Part of *Apostolic Church Order,* and other matter. 8. **X,** greatly expanded.
Sinodos of Alexandria	Sahidic Bohairic Arabic Ethiopic	1. *Apostolic Church Order.* 2. **X.** 3. Another version of **AC,** book 8. 4. *Canons of the Apostles.*
Clementine Octateuch	Arabic	1. *Testamentum Domini* **(TD).** 2-8. =Sinodos 1-4.
	Syriac	1, 2. =**TD.** 3-8. =Sinodos 1, 3, 4 (i.e. omitting **X,** except chapter 1).

[1] The following abbreviations which are constantly used hereafter should be noted:
A   Arabic version
AC *Apostolic Constitutions*
AT *Apostolic Tradition*
CH *Canons of Hippolytus*
E   Ethiopic version
JTS *Journal of Theological Studies*
L   Latin version
S   Sahidic Coptic version
SP *Studia Patristica*
TD *Testamentum Domini*
References to 'Bibliography' should be followed up on p.32 below.

Thus **X** appears several times over in these collections: as a separate document in the anonymous collection (no. 3), the Sinodos (no. 2), and the Arabic Octateuch (no. 3); much expanded, in **AC,** book 8, and in another version of **AC** 8 in the Sinodos (no. 3) and the Octateuch (no. 4); and in a different expansion, **TD,** in the Octateuch. In every case, it is associated with the *Apostolic Church Order,* a short treatise incorporating the 'Two Ways' from the *Didache* and setting out the requirements for the various orders of the clergy. Besides these sources, there is also an abridgment of **AC** known as the *Epitome,* and yet another rewriting of **X** called *The Canons of Hippolytus* (**CH**). In addition, a few fragments of **X** survive in Greek, the language in which it is presumed to have been originally written.

The Title of X

Various titles have been attached to **X.** In the 'Ochrid fragment',[1] an isolated passage in Greek, it is quoted as *Diataxeis ton hagion apostolon dia Hippolytou,* which is the title that the *Epitome* places before the equivalent of chapter 3 of **X,** adding *peri cheirotonias* after *apostolon.* This may well be the original title: *Ordinances of the holy apostles (about ordination) through Hippolytus.* However, Epiphanius of Salamis, writing *c.*375, quotes the *Didascalia* nine times as *Diataxis* (singular) and once as *Diataxeis* (plural)[2], which suggests that by his time the whole 'anonymous collection' was known by this title. (The Greek for **AC** is *Diatagai . . .*)

The title by which **X** is now known, *Apostolic Tradition,* only occurs in the sources as the last two words of the Latin version, which breaks off in the middle of a sentence (which may also have been the case with the Greek original); no existing manuscript actually bears this title.

The Authorship of X

As we have seen, the attribution of **X** to Hippolytus in the *Epitome* is supported by the title of the *Canons of Hippolytus;* and further support comes from archaeological evidence. In 1551 a statue was dug up in Rome (exactly where is unclear); though it bears no name, on its base it has a list of titles, many of which are universally accepted as genuine works of a considerable theologian named Hippolytus. Among them is a title, or titles, *PERI CHARISMATON/APOSTOLIKE PARADO/SIS* ('Of Spiritual Gifts/Apostolic Tradi/tion'), which could not for a long time be identified among the works of Hippolytus. This title again has a link with the *Epitome,* which applies the title *Didascalia ton hagion apostolon peri charismaton* to the two chapters preceding the title *Diataxeis . . .* quoted above. These two titles taken together may well refer to the same work or works as *Peri charismaton apostolike paradosis* on the statue.

In 1906 E. von der Goltz suggested that **X** was in fact the *Apostolic Tradition* of Hippolytus, hitherto believed lost. His suggestion was taken up and elaborated, first by W. Schwartz in 1910, and finally by R. H. Connolly[3] in 1916. It is now accepted by the great majority of scholars, though some prominent orientalists still have reservations. We may now refer to it as the *Apostolic Tradition* (**AT**).

1 Dix-Chadwick, page *c.*
2 *Haereses,* 45.4, 70.10-12, 75.6, 80.7.
3 Bibliography, no. 2.

Dates

The Hippolytus of the statue was active in Rome in the first part of the third century. There is no need to discuss here whether he is to be identified with either St. Hippolytus, a priest, martyred with pope Pontianus after 235 and commemorated on 13 August, or St. Hippolytus, bishop of Portus Romanus, martyred after 253 (22 August). Scholarly opinion seems to favour the former, if either. The popular picture of Hippolytus as an anti-pope seems to have been invented by J. J. I. Dollinger in 1853.[1]

Since **AT** was professedly written to guard 'the tradition which has remained until now' against recent inventions 'through ignorance or error', it has been ascribed to the early years of pope Callistus, an old enemy of Hippolytus, who succeeded in 217; but C. C. Richardson[2] has argued in favour of the early years of the previous pope, Zephyrinus, whom Hippolytus elsewhere describes as 'ignorant and illiterate and unskilled in church ordinances'.[3] On internal evidence, as H. Chadwick writes, 'the recovered church order is unquestionably a product of the first half of the third century'.[4]

The Contents

Chapters 1-14 (as numbered below) deal with ordinations (the *cheirotonia* of the title in the *Epitome*), and chapters 15-21 with the catechumenate and baptism. Chapter 21 ends with a short epilogue, which led W. H. Frere[5] to suggest that the treatise originally ended at this point. Certainly the remaining chapters are much less logically arranged. Their subject-matter includes the duties of deacons (22, 24, 34, 39), fasting (23, 33, 36), the *agape* (25-30), offerings of fruit (31, 32), private prayer (35, 41, 42), care of the consecrated elements (37, 38), and cemetery fees (40). This disorderly sequence suggests a gradual accumulation of separate units, rather than the systematic organization seen in chapters 1-21. (The order below is that of the Latin, with the gaps filled from the other versions, which differ among themselves.)

Even after making allowance for local modifications, **AT** is of incomparable importance as a source of information about church life and liturgy in the third century. It is 150 years earlier than any other surviving form of service. What remains uncertain is how far it is typical of life and liturgy *in Rome.* Some parts must be attributed to Hippolytus himself; and some scholars hold that, even if he wrote **AT** in Rome, the liturgy he describes is that of Alexandria, or alternatively, Syria. Certainly there is very little connection with later Roman services, but so little is known of the liturgies of the first three centuries that any attempt to determine the place of origin of **AT** is hazardous in the extreme.

On the other hand, it is clear that its *influence* was widely felt in the East: Asia Minor, Syria, Egypt, and Ethiopia all treated it as an authoritative document, to be copied and re-edited. A version of its anaphora is still in use in Ethiopia today.

[1] Hanssens, I. pp.313-6.
[2] Bibliography, no. 16.
[3] *Philosophoumena,* 9.11.
[4] Dix-Chadwick, pages *g, h.*
[5] Bibliography, no. 8.

The Manuscripts

Of the versions of **AT,** as opposed to the rewritings, by far the oldest is the Latin, as this table shows:

	LATIN	SAHIDIC	ARABIC	ETHIOPIC	BOHAIRIC
Translated	c.350[1]	before 700[2]	1295	after 1295	1804
Oldest MS	c.500	1006	14th cent.	15th cent.	after 1804

The Latin (**L**) is a closely literal translation by someone who was not fully conversant with the contents (A. F. Walls suggests 'an Arian and Gothic origin'[3], J. M. Hanssens 'a Visigothic ecclesiastic of the Cisdanubian provinces'[4]). Unfortunately, it is far from complete: there is one gap in the manuscript of six pages, and two gaps of two pages each.

The Sahidic (**S**) also seems to be fairly close to the Greek, but it lacks the text of the prayers, and has some post-Nicene readings. One page is lacking, which can be supplied from the Bohairic. The latter is a translation from the Sahidic, of little interest.

The Arabic (**A**) has also been translated from the Sahidic, and adds little of importance.

The Ethiopic (**E**) is one step further still from the original, having been made from an Arabic version which included the prayers; but it is the fullest of all, containing the whole of the original and a good deal of material not found in the other versions. The text, however, is often confused.

Of the works derived from **AT, AC** is thought to have been compiled c.360-375 in Syria, **TD** in the fourth or fifth century, possibly in Asia Minor, and **CH** c.335 in Egypt. The manuscripts, of course, are much later. Though all three were written in Greek, **TD** has survived only in Syriac, Arabic, and Ethiopic, **CH** only in Arabic. Dix and, to a less extent, Botte, make much use in their editions of these derivative documents, especially **TD,** which Dix thought to be based on a very good manuscript of **AT**. But for this edition, which does not attempt to reconstitute the original, they are less relevant, and they are only quoted when their evidence is crucial. In any case, when **AC** or **TD** offers an easier reading or a more logical sequence, it cannot be assumed that they are preserving the original text: rather, they may simply be trying, like modern editors, to make better sense of a difficult passage.

This Edition

L has been taken as the fundamental text, except in the four chapters (3, 11, 23, 36) where the original Greek is available. The gaps in **L** have been filled from **S**, or failing that, from **E** or the Bohairic. Also, at some points where the Latin is erroneous or unintelligible, it has been corrected from one or other of the oriental versions. All these insertions or alterations are printed in italics, and their source is indicated in the footnotes. The portions of the text printed in roman are all from **L**. Words in brackets have been added as being necessary in English to complete the sense.

[1] Bibliography, no. 23 (p.337).
[2] Hanssens, I. p.35.
[3] Bibliography, no. 19.
[4] Hanssens, II. p.16.

The translation of the Coptic, Arabic, and Ethiopic versions has been made after comparison of the Latin renderings by Botte and Hanssens and the English of Horner.

Liturgical *text*, as distinguished from *rubrics, instructions* and *descriptions,* has been slightly indented, so that it can be readily discerned. Congregational or responsive material has been further indented.

The division into chapters follows that of Botte, which is closely based on that of the versions. The numbering of the chapters also follows Botte's; Dix's numbering is added in brackets, since it is still widely used.

The textual apparatus is confined to readings of real importance. A fuller selection of variants may be found in Dix or Botte, where the complexity of the situation is plainly visible. The footnotes constitute the apparatus on their own, and are clearly distinguished from the commentary material above them on each page

BIBLIOGRAPHY

Modern editions

B. Botte, *La Tadition Apostolique de saint Hippolyte* (Münster, [1]1963, [2]1972). French translation; Latin text and composite Oriental text in Latin

G. Dix, *The Apostolic Tadition of St. Hippolytus* (London, 1937; 2nd edn, with preface. and corrections by H. Chadwick, S.P.C.K., London, 1968 (cited as Dix-Chadwick)) English translation; Latin and Greek texts; and other sources in apparatus.

G. Horner, *The Statutes of the Apostles* (Oxford, 1904). Arabic and Ethiopic texts; English translations of **S, A,** and **E.**

J. M. Hanssens, *La Liturgie d'Hippolyte* vol. 1 (Rome, 1959; 2nd edn. Rome, 1965). Massive documentation. Vol. II (Rome, 1970). Latin translation of all relevant texts.

L E. Tidner, *Didascaliae apostolorum canonum ecclesiasticorum traditionis apostolicae vesiones latinae* (Berlin, 1963).

S W. Till and J. Leipoldt, *Der koptische Text de Kirchenordnung Hippolyts* (Berlin, 1954).

A J. & A. Perier, *Les 127 Canons des apôtres* (Paris, 1912, *Patrologia Orientalis* 8. 4).

E H. Duensing, *Der aethiopische Text der Kirchenordnung des Hippolyt,* (Göttingen, 1946).

AC F. X. Funk, *Didascalia et Constitutiones Apostolorum,* 2 vols. (Paderborn, 1905).

CH R. G. Coquin, *Canones Hippolyti* (Paris, 1966, *Patrologia Orientalis* 31.2).

TD J. Cooper and A. J. Maclean, *The Testament of our Lord* (Edinburgh, 1902).

A bibliography of books and articles is to be found on p.32 below.

THE TEXT

(APOSTOLIC TRADITION)[1]

1. We have set down those things which were worthy of note about the gifts which God has bestowed on man from the beginning according to his own will, presenting to himself that image which had gone astray. And now, led on by love[2] for all the saints, we have proceeded to the summit of the tradition which *befits*[3] the churches, in order that those who have been well *taught*[4] by our exposition may guard that tradition which has remained up to now, and by recognising it may remain firm—because of that backsliding or error which was recently invented through ignorance—and that those who are ignorant (since the holy Spirit bestows perfect grace on those who believe rightly) may know how those who preside over the Church should hand down and guard all things.

OF BISHOPS

2. Let him be ordained bishop who has been chosen by[5] all the people; and when he has been named and accepted by all, let the people assemble, together with the presbytery and those bishops who are present, on the Lord's day. When all give consent, they shall lay hands on him, and the presbytery shall stand by and be still. And all shall keep silence, praying in their hearts for the descent of the Spirit; after which one of the bishops present, being asked by all, shall lay his hand on him who is being ordained bishop, and pray, saying thus:

COMMENTARY

Title] See Introduction, page 4.

1 E places this prologue between chs. 30 and 31, for no apparent reason. Both **E** and **L** are confused, and translation is unusually difficult. The Syriac Octateuch confirms two of **E**'s readings against **L**; Dix ignores this source, despite Connolly's article (Bibliog. 3).

> Worthy of note] **L**: *verba digne;* Dix suggests *'verbi digna'*, which I have translated, as being equivalent to a possible Greek original *'axiologa'*.
> Gifts] **AC** and Syriac Octateuch: *charismata,* i.e. spiritual gifts.
> Love for all the saints] Col. 1.4 or Eph. 1.15.
> Befits] Suggested by W. H. Frere (Bibliography, 8, p.330; not 32, as in Dix).

2 By all the people] E. C. Ratcliff (Bibliography, 13) strongly supports the reading 'from' (**S, A, E**); at that stage each order was conferred for life, so that priests and deacons would be ineligible.
> He would also add 'as we appointed above' (**S, A, E, AC**), cf. chs.7 and 8.

NOTES (i.e. apparatus footnotes)

[1] All chapter-headings are illegible in **L**; those in the text are supplied from other sources, usually from **S**, those in brackets by the editor.
[2] So **E** and Syriac Octateuch; **L** adds 'which he had'.
[3] So **E** and Syriac Octateuch (=*kathekei*); **L**: 'catechizes' (=*katechei*).
[4] So **E**; **L**: 'led' (*ducti,* wrongly, for *docti*).
[5] **S, A. E**: 'from'.

THE PRAYER FOR ORDINATION OF A BISHOP[1]

3. *God and Father of our Lord Jesus Christ, Father of mercies and God of all comfort, you dwell on high and look on that which is lowly; you know all things before they come to pass; you gave ordinances in the Church through the word of your grace; you foreordained from the beginning a race of righteous men* from[2] *Abraham; you appointed princes and priests, and did not leave your sanctuary without a ministry. From the beginning of the age it was your good pleasure to be* glorified[3] *in those whom you have chosen: now pour forth that power which is from you, of the princely Spirit which*[4] *you granted* through *your beloved Son Jesus Christ to your holy apostles*[4] *who established the Church in every place as your sanctuary, to the unceasing glory and praise of your name.*

[5]*You who know the hearts of all, bestow upon this your servant, whom you have chosen for* [6]*the episcopate, to feed your holy* flock *and to exercise*[6] *the high-priesthood before you blamelessly, serving night and day; to propitiate your countenance unceasingly, and to offer to you the gifts of your holy Church; and by the spirit of high-priesthood to have the power to forgive sins according to your command, to confer orders according to your bidding, to loose every bond according to the power which you gave to the apostles, to please you in gentleness and a pure heart, offering to you a sweet-smelling savour; through your child Jesus Christ our Lord, with whom be glory and power and honour to you,*[7] *with the holy Spirit*[8], *both now and to the ages of ages. Amen.*

---

3 These ordination prayers have virtually no connection with the next earliest examples, those in the Leonine Sacramentary. As expanded in **AC,** they were adopted in the Coptic rite. The double laying-on of hands is an example of what A. F. Walls (Bibliography, 20) calls 'harmonized diversity'. **TD** provides a prayer for each.

God and Father] 2 Cor. 1.3.   You dwell] Ps. 113.5, 6.
You know] Susanna 42.   The word] Acts 20.22.
Princely Spirit] Ps. 51.12 (LXX, 50.14: *pneumati hegemonikoi)*.
You who know] Acts 1.24   Bestow] Isa. 42.1.
The episcopate] The *Epitome* has accidentally omitted a line.
To forgive] John 20.23; Acts 1.26; Mt. 18.18.
A sweet-smelling savour] Eph. 5.2.   Child] Acts 3.13; *Didache,* 9.
Doxology] **L**'s 'to Father and Son' is superfluous after 'with whom . . . to you'.
For further details of the functions of a bishop, see chs.4-9, 11, 20-22, 25, 26, 28, 31, 32, 39, 40.

---

[1] The title and text of chapter 3 are to be found in the *Epitome,* which here reproduces the original Greek, not the version of **AC.**

[2] **L** omits *ab* before *Abraham.*

[3] **L:** 'given' (*dari,* =*dothenai,* wrongly for *doxasthenai).*

[4-4] So *Epitome;* **L:** 'whom you gave to your beloved Son Jesus Christ, which he gave to your holy apostles . . .'

[5] **L** adds 'Father' .

[6] So **L;** *Epitome:* 'for your holy episcopate and to exercise . . .

[7] **L** adds 'to Father and Son' (cf. chapters 4, 6, 7).

[8] **E** adds 'in the holy Church' (cf. chapters 4, 6, 7).

4. And when he has been made bishop, all shall offer the kiss of peace, greeting him[1] because he has been made worthy.[1] Then the deacons shall present the offering to him; and he, laying his hands on it with all the presbytery, shall give thanks, saying:

> The Lord be with you;[2]

and all shall say:

> And with your spirit.
> Up with your hearts.
> We have them with the Lord.
> Let us give thanks to the Lord.
> It is fitting and right.

And then he shall continue thus:

> We render thanks to you, O God, through your beloved child Jesus Christ, whom in the last times you sent to us as saviour and redeemer and angel of your will; who is your inseparable Word, through whom you made all things, and in whom you were well pleased. You sent him from heaven into the Virgin's womb; and, conceived in the womb, he was made flesh and was manifested as your Son, being born of the holy Spirit and the Virgin. Fulfilling your will and gaining for you a holy people, he stretched out his hands when he should suffer, that he might release from suffering those who have believed in you.

> And when he was betrayed to voluntary suffering that he might destroy death, and break the bonds of the devil, and tread down hell, and shine upon the righteous, and fix a term, and manifest the

---

4 All versions treat chs. 3 and 4 as one, but modern editions print the eucharist as a separate chapter. The language of the thanksgiving is studied in an important article by R. H. Connolly (Bibliography, 5), stressing especially parallels with Irenaeus; the language of the first section is characteristic of Hippolytus. The stress on redemption argues against an Egyptian origin, while the anamnesis section is faithfully reproduced in **AC,** and is the only part that appears to have influenced the Roman Canon. The absence of the Sanctus would indicate an early date for an Eastern anaphora, but at Rome there is no evidence for its inclusion until c.450 (L. Chavoutier, in *Sacris Erudiri* 11 (1960) pp.136-92). Ratcliff thought that **AT** 'was considerably revised after it left Hippolytus' hand'; what we have 'is not Hippolytus' original composition, but an edition of it current in the last quarter of the fourth century' (review of Botte's edition, *JTS*, n.s. 15 (1964) pp.402-7).

Because he has been made worthy] J. A. Jungmann translates 'that . . .' (*quia*); *'vix recte'* (Tidner).

Hands] **S, A, E** all read 'hand' (singular).

The Lord be with you] The earliest recorded occurrence of this dialogue. The first couplet is native to Egypt.

Up with your hearts] cf Cyprian, *De orat. Dom.* 31, who also spells it *'susum'*.

The last times] Gal. 4.4. Angel of your will] Is. 9.5 (LXX), 9.6 (AV).

Through whom . . .] John 1.3. Gaining] Acts 20.28.

A holy people] 1 Peter 2.9. Voluntary suffering] cf. Justin, *Dial.* 41.

Fix a term] Connolly suggests 'for the resurrection'; Botte 'fix the rule (of faith)'; Dix 'the limit (probably of hell)'.

1-1 **S** omits 'because . . . worthy'.

2 **S,E** add 'all'.

resurrection, he took bread and gave thanks to you, saying, 'Take, eat; this is my body, which shall be broken for you'. Likewise also the cup, saying, 'This is my blood, which is shed for you; when you do this, you make my remembrance'.

Remembering therefore his death and resurrection, we offer to you the bread and the cup, giving you thanks because you have held us worthy to stand before you and minister to you. And we ask that you would send your holy Spirit upon the offering of your holy Church; that, [1]gathering (her) into one, you would grant to [2]all who partake of the holy things[2] (to partake) for the fullness of the holy Spirit[1] for the strengthening of faith in truth, that we may praise and glorify you through your child Jesus Christ, through whom be glory and honour to you, [3]with the holy Spirit, in your holy Church, both now and to the ages of ages. Amen.

OF THE OFFERING OF OIL[4]

5. If anyone offers oil, (the bishop) shall render thanks in the same way as for the offering of bread and wine, not saying it word for word, but to similar effect, saying:

O God, sanctifier of this oil, as you give health[5] to those who are anointed[6] and receive that with which you anointed kings, priests, and prophets, so may it give strength to all those who taste it, and health to all that are anointed[6] with it.

Broken] NB future (so also Ambrose, *De Sacr.*, 4.21); **AC** has *'thruptomenon'* (so also Codex Bezae); textus receptus, *'klomenon'*. The narrative is a combination of Matthew and Paul (cf. Justin).

When you do this] **L**: *facitis*=Greek *'poieite'*, which could be indicative or imperative. The original probably read *'Do this for* my remembrance', as in Luke and 1 Cor. Dix has a note on anamnesis (pp.73-5), but it should be noted that the sermon from which he gives a long quotation is not by Hippolytus (see Connolly, *JTS* 46 (1945), pp.192-200; this applies also to the quotations on pp.xxxiii, 78, 85).

Send your holy Spirit] Controversy has raged over the authenticity of this epiclesis. **L** is almost untranslatable as it stands; **AC** and **TD** have paraphrased it in their different ways. Dix and Ratcliff held it to be a fourth-century interpolation; Connolly accepted it as third-century. As an invocation on behalf of the worshippers, not specifying the effect on the elements, it seems quite credible.

Gathering (her)] John 11.52.

5 A Greek version of this prayer is quoted in Dix-Chadwick, page *d.* Sarapion has a 'Prayer over the offerings of oils and waters', also placed after the anaphora. Cf. the blessing of chrism on Maundy Thursday in the Gregorian Sacramentary (Jasper & Cuming, *Prayers of the Eucharist* (Collins, 1975), p.109): and see Dix, p.xlv, note * for a further possible parallel.

1-1 **TD**: 'Grant to all who partake of the holy things to be united with you for filling with holy Spirit'.

2-2 *Sanctis* ('the holy things') could be masculine: 'all the saints who partake'.

3 **L** adds 'to Father and Son'.

4 Title from **E**; **S** omits the whole chapter.

5 Dix and Botte conjecture 'holiness' (*hagiasma*) for 'health' (*hygiasma*); but two lines later the reading 'health' is undoubtedly correct.

6 So **E**; **L** has misread *chriomenois* ('anointed') as *chromenois* ('using').

(OF THE OFFERING OF CHEESE AND OLIVES)[1]

6. Likewise, if anyone offers cheese and olives, he shall say thus: ·

> Sanctify this milk which has been coagulated, coagulating us also to your love. Make this fruit of the olive not to depart from your sweetness, which is an example of your richness which you have poured from the tree for life to those who hope in you.

But in every blessing shall be said:

> To you be glory, to the Father and the Son with the holy Spirit, in the holy Church, both now and always and to all the ages of ages.[2]

OF PRESBYTERS

7. (Dix 8). And when a presbyter is ordained, the bishop shall lay his hand on his head, the presbyters also touching him; and he shall say according to what was said above, as we said before about the bishop, praying and saying:

> God and Father of our Lord Jesus Christ, look upon this your servant, and impart the Spirit of grace and counsel of the presbyterate, that he may help and govern your people with a pure heart; just as you looked upon your chosen people, and commanded Moses to choose presbyters whom you filled with your Spirit which you granted to your servant. And now, Lord, grant the Spirit of your grace to be preserved unfailingly in us, and make us worthy to minister to you [3]in faith and in simplicity of heart, praising you through your child Christ Jesus; through whom be glory and power to you [4]with the holy Spirit, in the holy Church, both now and to the ages of ages. Amen.

---

6 This chapter was known to the author of **TD,** who quotes the phrase 'which is an example of your richness'. It was therefore presumably in the original Greek, but it is odd that **E** does not include it.

The doxology is of a form in which 'to Father and Son' is perfectly appropriate (cf. ch.3). For the text of the spurious communion prayers, see Dix, pp.11, 12, and 80.

7 Dix (Bibliography 7) adopts a suggestion of C. H. Turner's that the first part of the prayer for a bishop (ch.3) is to be said as the first part of this prayer also, but this is thought unlikely by Botte, Ratcliff, and Walls. If Ratcliff's restoration of 'as we appointed above' in ch.2 is accepted, there is no problem here.

> Presbyterate] Tidner, the most recent editor of **L,** reads *'praesbyterii';* Hauler, the first editor, read *'praesbyteris',* which gives an inferior sense.
>
> Help and govern] 1 Cor. 12.28; 'the corporate presbyterate' is 'the governing body of the Church' (Dix, Bibliography, 6, p.218). Dix suggests that a clause has fallen out after 'heart' (*ibid.*, p.218, n.1).
>
> To choose presbyters] i.e., elders; Num. 11.16.
>
> Make us worthy] i.e., all the presbyters present.
>
> Simplicity] Eph. 6.5.

For further details of the functions of a presbyter, see chs. 2, 8, 21-3, 25, 28, 39.

---

[1] This chapter is found only in **L.** The title is conjectural, the original being indecipherable.

[2] **E** here inserts five spurious eucharistic prayers (Dix 7).

[3] **E, AC, TD** all read 'filled'; **L** may have misread *plesthentes* ('filled') as *peisthentes* ('believing').

[4] **L** adds 'to Father and Son'.

OF DEACONS[1]

8. (Dix 9). But when a deacon is ordained, let him be chosen according to what was said above, the bishop alone laying on hands, in the same way as we also directed above. In the ordination of a deacon, the bishop alone shall lay on hands, because he is not being ordained to the priesthood, but to the service of the bishop, to do what is ordered by him. For he does not share in the counsel of the clergy, but administers and informs the bishop of what is fitting; he does not receive the common spirit of seniority in which the presbyters share, but that which is entrusted to him under the bishop's authority. For this reason the bishop alone shall ordain a deacon; but on a presbyter the presbyters alone shall lay hands, because of the common and like spirit of their order. For a presbyter has authority only to receive; he has not authority to give. For this reason he does not ordain the clergy, but at the ordination of a presbyter he seals, while the bishop ordains.

Over a deacon, then, (the bishop) shall say thus:

God, who created all things and ordered them by your Word, Father of our Lord Jesus Christ, whom you sent to serve your will and make known to us your desire, give the holy Spirit of grace and caring and diligence to this your servant whom you have chosen to serve your Church and to present[2]

in your holy of holies that which is offered to you by your appointed high-priest to the glory of your name; that, serving blamelessly and purely, he may attain the rank of a higher order, and praise and glorify you through your Son Jesus Christ our Lord; through whom be glory and power and praise to you, with the holy Spirit, now and always and to the ages of ages. Amen.

8   Ordained] **S** has a different verb, *kathistanai,* which means 'appoint', and may perhaps be more accurate.

He is not being ordained] This passage seems to have influenced later Gallican practice (Dix, p.xlvi).

Seniority] For the justification of this rendering, see D. Powell, *'Ordo Presbyterii', JTS,* n.s.26 (1975), pp.290-328.

He seals] i.e., he confirms, or ratifies; cf. John 3.33. This custom was unknown in the East, which has led to confusion in **A** and **E.**

He does not ordain] **S** again has *kathistanai.*

Serve] Greek: *diakonein.*

To present] cf. ch.4, 'The deacons shall present the offering'.

A higher order] cf. 1 Tim. 3.13, 'a good standing', and Leonine Sacramentary, *'potiora'* ('higher things').

For further details of the functions of a deacon, see chs.21-5, 28, 34, 39.

[1] Title from **S.**

[2] **L** breaks off here. The rest of the prayer is supplied from **E;** it is lacking from **S,** like all the prayers.

OF CONFESSORS[1]

9. *(Dix 10). But a confessor, if he was in chains for the name of the Lord, shall not have hands laid on him for the diaconate or the presbyterate, for he has the honour of the presbyterate by his confession. But if he is appointed bishop, hands shall be laid on him.*

But if there is a confessor who was not brought before the authorities, nor punished with chains, nor shut up in prison, nor condemned to any other penalty, but has only been derided on occasion for the name of our Lord, and punished with a domestic punishment: if he confessed, let hands be laid on him for any order of which he is worthy.

And the bishop shall give thanks according to what we said above. It is not at all necessary for him to utter the same words as we said above, as though reciting them from memory, when giving thanks to God; but let each pray according to his ability. If indeed anyone has the ability to pray at length and with a solemn prayer, it is good. But if anyone, when he prays, utters a brief prayer, do not prevent him. Only, he must pray what is sound and orthodox.

OF WIDOWS[1]

10 *(Dix 11). When a widow is appointed, she is not ordained, but is chosen by name. If her husband has been dead a long time, let her not be taken on trust; even if she is old, let her be tested for a time, for often the passions grow old with him who makes a place for them in himself. A widow shall be appointed by word only, and shall join the rest. But hands shall not be laid on her, because she does not offer the offering, nor has she a liturgical duty. Ordination is for the clergy, on account of their liturgical duties; but a widow is appointed for prayer, which belongs to all.*

---

9   We said above] i.e., in ch. 4; this is not contradicted by the following sentence, as some have supposed.

    It is not at all necessary] **A** and **E** omit 'not at all', reflecting the practice of an era when it was no longer the custom for the celebrant to compose his own thanksgiving.

    According to his ability] cf. Justin, *Apol.* 67.5, *'hose dynamis autoi'*.

    At length] Literally, 'sufficiently'; cf. Justin, *Apol.* 65.3, *'epi polu'*.

    Brief] Literally, 'measured'; contrasted with 'at length' and with 'solemn'.

10   The order of chapters 10-14 varies in the different versions; see the table in Botte (p.xxx). Easton, Dix, and Botte all adopt the order of **A** and **E**, which has therefore been retained in this translation; but the order of **S** (readers, subdeacons, widows, virgins) is the most logical, and there seems no good reason for departing from this source.

    By name] A widow is simply nominated.

    For often . . . himself] **CH** has this phrase in ch.16, at the end of the fifth paragraph (Dix, p.lxxviii).

---

[1] Chapters 9 and 10 are taken from **S.**

OF A READER[1]

11. *(Dix 12). A reader is appointed by the bishop giving him the book, for he does not have hands laid on him.*

OF A VIRGIN[2]

12. *(Dix 13). Hands shall not be laid on a virgin: her choice alone makes her a virgin.*

OF A SUBDEACON[2]

13. *(Dix 14). Hands shall not be laid on a subdeacon, but he shall be named in order that he may follow the deacons.*

OF GIFTS OF HEALING[2]

14. *(Dix 15). If anyone says, 'I have received a gift of healing by a revelation', hands shall not be laid on him, for the facts themselves will show whether he has spoken the truth.*

OF NEWCOMERS TO THE FAITH[2]

15. *(Dix 16.1-8). Those who come forward for the first time to hear the word shall first be brought to the teachers before all the people arrive, and shall be questioned about their reason for coming to the faith. And those who have brought them shall bear witness about them, whether they are capable of hearing the word. They shall be questioned about their state of life: has he a wife? Is he the slave of a believer? Does his master allow him? Let him hear the word. If his master does not bear witness about him that he is a good man, he shall be rejected. If his master is a heathen, teach him to please his master, that there be no scandal. If any man has a wife, or a woman a husband, they shall be taught to be contented, the man with his wife and the woman with her husband. But if any man is not living with a wife, he shall be instructed not to fornicate, but to take a wife lawfully or remain as he is. If anyone is possessed by a demon, he shall not hear the word of teaching until he is pure.*

OF CRAFTS AND PROFESSIONS[2]

16. *(Dix 16.9-25). Inquiry shall be made about the crafts and professions of those who are brought for instruction. If a man is a brothel-keeper, let him cease or be rejected. If anyone is a sculptor or a painter, let them be instructed not to make idols; let them cease or be rejected. If anyone is an actor or gives theatrical performances, let him cease or be rejected. He who teaches children had best cease; but if he has no craft, let him have permission.*

---

13   Follow] Greek: *akoloutheo;* acolytes ('followers') are not known as a separate order before 250.

14   Gift of healing] Exorcists are not known as a separate order before 250.

15   The teachers] **TD** adds 'at the house', which Dix thinks is original.
Remain as he is] 1 Cor. 7.40.

16   The list of forbidden occupations varies from version to version; e.g., **A** and **E** leave out the references to charioteers and gladiators, which did not apply in their part of the world (Dix, p.25 note 10). Schoolmasters are included because they had to teach pagan myths; **E** restricts the condemnation to those who teach worldly knowledge, **A** omits the whole sentence. Cf. Tertullian, *De Idololatria* (*c.*211-2), ch.10.

---

[1] Chapter 11 is taken from the *Epitome,* which here quotes the original Greek.
[2] Chapters 12-20 and the first part of chapter 21 are taken from **S.**

Similarly, a charioteer who competes in the games, or goes to them, let him cease or be rejected. One who is a gladiator or teaches gladiators to fight, or one who fights with beasts in the games, or a public official employed on gladiatorial business, let him cease or be rejected.

If anyone is a priest, or keeper, of idols, let him cease or be rejected.

A soldier under authority shall not kill a man. If he is ordered to, he shall not carry out the order; nor shall he take the oath. If he is unwilling, let him be rejected. He who has the power of the sword, or is a magistrate of a city who wears the purple, let him cease or be rejected. Catechumens or believers who want to become soldiers should be rejected, because they have despised God.

A prostitute, a profligate, a eunuch, or anyone else who does things of which it is a shame to speak, let them be rejected, for they are impure. Neither shall a magician be brought for examination. A charmer, an astrologer, a diviner, an interpreter of dreams, a mountebank, a cutter of fringes of clothes, or a maker of phylacteries, let them be rejected.

A man's concubine, if she is his slave and has reared her children and remained faithful to him alone, may be a hearer; otherwise, let her be rejected. Let any man who has a concubine cease, and take a wife lawfully; but if he is unwilling, let him be rejected.

If we have left anything out, the facts themselves will teach you; for we all have the Spirit of God.

OF THE TIME OF HEARING THE WORD AFTER (EXAMINATION OF) CRAFTS AND PROFESSIONS[1]

17. *Catechumens shall continue to hear the word for three years. But if a man is keen, and perseveres well in the matter, the time shall not be judged, but only his conduct.*

OF THE PRAYER OF THOSE WHO HEAR THE WORD[1]

18. *When the teacher has finished giving instruction, let the catechumens pray by themselves, separated from the faithful; and let the women, whether faithful or catechumens, stand by themselves in some place in the church when they pray. And when they have finished praying, they shall not give the Peace, for their kiss is not yet holy. But let only the faithful greet*

Take the oath] Once again **A** and **E** omit a process with which they are not familiar. A eunuch] Botte (p.37 note 7) takes this as meaning 'a homosexual'.
A shame to speak] Eph. 5.12.
Fringes of clothes] **S** adds 'who are stammerers'(!). Botte conjectures 'coin-trimmers', but Chadwick points out that the context is the practice of magic; hence the rendering in the text (see Dix-Chadwick, pages *m, n*).
The Spirit of God] 1 Cor. 7.40.

18 In the church] Dix's statement (p.lv) that 'everywhere in the *Apostolic Tradition* "the Church" means *the congregation, not the building*' is not borne out by this passage, nor by similar expressions in chs.21, 35, 39, and 41, where *'ecclesia'* can equally, or more probably does, mean 'the building'. His argument on p.lv is therefore unsoundly based.
Their kiss . . . holy] Rom. 16.16; 1 Cor. 16.20; 2 Cor. 13.12.

---

[1] See footnote 2 on p.15.

one another, men with men and women with women; but the men shall not greet the women. And let all the women cover their heads with a hood, but (not) just with a piece of linen, for that is no veil.

OF LAYING HANDS ON THE CATECHUMENS[1]

19. *After their prayer, when the teacher has laid hands on the catechumens, he shall pray and dismiss them. Whether the teacher is a cleric or a layman, let him act thus.*

If a catechumen is arrested for the name of the Lord, let him not be in two minds about his witness. For if he suffers violence and is killed (before he has received baptism) for the forgiveness of his sins, he will be justified, for he has received baptism in his blood.

OF THOSE WHO WILL RECEIVE BAPTISM[1]

20. *And when those who are to receive baptism are chosen, let their life be examined: have they lived good lives when they were catechumans? Have they honoured the widows? Have they visited the sick? Have they done every kind of good work? And when those who brought them bear witness to each: 'He has', let them hear the gospel.*

From the time that they were set apart, let hands be laid on them daily while they are exorcized. And when the day of their baptism approaches, the bishop shall exorcize each one of them, in order that he may know whether he is pure. And if anyone is not good or not pure, let him be put aside, because he has not heard the word with faith, for it is impossible that the Alien should hide himself for ever.

Those who are to be baptized should be instructed to bathe[2] and wash themselves on the Thursday. And if a woman is in her period, let her be put aside, and receive baptism another day. Those who are to receive baptism shall fast on the Friday. On the Saturday those who are to receive baptism shall be gathered in one place at the bishop's decision. They shall all be told to pray and kneel. And he shall lay his hand on them and exorcize all alien spirits, that they may flee out of them and never return

---

19 (Before he has received baptism)] These words are supplied from **E.** The syntax of **S** suggests that their equivalent has fallen out at this point.

20 Chosen] Baptismal candidates at Rome were called *'electi'.*
Honoured the widows] 1 Tim. 5.3.
The Alien] The Greek word was almost certainly *'allotrios'*, which was used of the Devil; cf. below, and chs. 21, 38, 42A, and Justin, *Dial.* 20.
Thursday] It is generally assumed that Hippolytus is describing a baptism at Easter, though he never actually says so. Tertullian speaks of baptism at Easter, Pentecost, or any time *(De Baptismo,* 20).
Shall fast on the Friday] cf. *Didache* 7; Justin, *Apol.* 61.2; Tertullian, *De Bapt.,* 20.
Flee] This clause reads like a quotation from the actual words of the service: 'Flee out of them and never return!' Cf. Mark 9.25.

---

[1] See footnote 2 on p.15.
[2] **S** adds 'and make themselves free' (not in **A, E, TD**). This is probably due to a scribal error convincingly explained by Botte (p.43, n.7).

into them. And when he has finished exorcizing them, he shall breathe on their faces; and when he has signed their foreheads, ears, and noses, he shall raise them up.

And they shall spend the whole night in vigil; they shall be read to and instructed. Those who are to be baptized shall not bring with them any other thing, except what each brings for the eucharist. For it is suitable that he who has been made worthy should offer an offering then.

OF THE CONFERRING OF HOLY BAPTISM[1]

21. *At the time when the cock crows, first let prayer be made over the water. Let the water be flowing in the font or poured over it. Let it be thus unless there is some necessity; if the necessity is permanent and urgent, use what water you can find. They shall take off their clothes. Baptize the little ones first. All those who can speak for themselves shall do so. As for those who cannot speak for themselves, their parents or someone from their family shall speak for them. Then baptize the men, and lastly the women, who shall have loosened all their hair, and laid down the gold and silver ornaments which they have on them. Let no-one take any alien object down into the water.*

And at the time fixed for baptizing, the bishop shall give thanks over the oil, which he puts in a vessel: one calls it 'oil of thanksgiving'. And he shall also take other oil and exorcize it: one calls it 'oil of exorcism'. And a deacon takes the oil of exorcism and stands on the priest's left; and another deacon takes the oil of thanksgiving and stands on the priest's right. And when the priest takes each one of those who are to receive baptism, he shall bid him renounce, saying:

I renounce you, Satan, and all your service and all your works.

And when each one has renounced all this, he shall anoint him with the oil of exorcism, saying to him:

Let every[2] *spirit depart far from you.*

Breathe] John 20.22.

Signed] i.e., with the sign of the cross; literally, 'sealed'.

The whole night] cf. Tertullian, *De Bapt.*, 20.

21 Prayer . . . the water] cf. Cyprian, *Letter 70.*

Font] Greek (in **S**): *kolumbethra* = 'a swimming-bath, tank'.

Little ones] cf. Tertullian, *De Bapt.*, 18.

Loosened all their hair] 'A custom directly drawn from Jewish lustrations' (Dix-Chadwick, page *m;* and see articles by Gavin, Van Unnik, and Werblowsky listed on pages *o* and *p*). Knots were 'a favourite seat of demons' (Werblowsky, p.99), or loosening was merely to ensure that all the hair got wet.

Alien object] i.e., an object in the power of the Devil; see ch.20, above.

Renounce] In Eastern baptismal rites the renunciation (*apotaxis*) is made facing west, and is followed by an act of adherence to Christ (*syntaxis*) made facing east (see, e.g., Cyril of Jerusalem, *Cat. Myst.*, 1.4, 9). **TD** and **CH** have introduced these ceremonies (Dix, p.35, 10*a* and 11*a*).

Service] Greek: probably *'pompe'* (Botte, p.47 note 5); cf. Tertullian, *De Corona*, 3; Cyril, *Cat. Myst.*, 1.5.

---

[1] See footnote 2 on p.15.

[2] **A, CH** add 'evil'; **E** adds 'impure'; **TD** adds both words.

And in this way he shall hand him over naked to the bishop or the priest who stands by the water to baptize. In the same way a deacon shall descend with him into the water and say, helping him to say:
*   I believe in one God, the Father almighty . . .*[1]
And he who receives shall say according to all this:
*   I believe in this way.*
And the giver,[2]

having his hand placed on his head, shall baptize him once.

And then he shall say:
    Do you believe in Christ Jesus, the Son of God, who was born from the holy Spirit from the Virgin Mary, and was crucified under Pontius Pilate, and died,[3] and rose again on the third day alive from the dead, and ascended into heaven, and sits at the right hand of the Father, and will come to judge the living and the dead?

And when he has said, 'I believe', he shall be baptized again.

And he shall say again:
    Do you believe in the holy Spirit and the holy Church and the resurrection of the flesh?
[4]Then he who is being baptized shall say, 'I believe', and thus he shall be baptized a third time.

The Father almighty] 'All that follows . . . has nothing to do with the *Tradition'* (Botte, p.49 note 1). The text of the interpolations in **S, A, E** is as follows:
    and in his only-begotten Son Jesus Christ our Lord and Saviour, and in his holy Spirit who makes all things alive, the Trinity of one substance, one Godhead, one Lordship, one kingdom, one faith, one baptism in the holy, catholic, and apostolic Church, one eternal life. Amen.
And the giver] **S, A, E** continue: 'shall lay his hand on the receiver's head and dip him three times while he confesses each time'.
And then he shall say] The interpolation in **S, A, E** has suppressed a triple interrogation, of which the second and third questions have been preserved by **L,** which obviously began:
    'Do you believe in God the Father almighty? And he who is being baptized shall also say, I believe. And at once the giver . . .'
This is in fact the reading of **TD. S, A, E** then proceed with a further interpolation (Dix, pp.lx, lxi; for a comparison of **L** and **TD,** see Dix, pp.lxvii–lxix).
He shall be baptized] Dix suggests that here and after the third question the word *'baptizetur'* should be given a middle sense, 'he shall baptize himself' (*Theology of Confirmation,* p.13).
And the holy Church] Dix and Botte both prefer the reading of **S, A, E:** 'in the holy Church', but D. L. Holland (Bibliography, 9) argues convincingly for the text of **L** ('and').
The resurrection of the flesh] **L, A, E** have these words; Bohairic, **CH, TD** omit them.

---

[1] **S, A, E** (but not **L, CH, TD**) add several clauses obviously later than the council of Constantinople (A.D. 381); see Dix, p.35.
[2] **L** begins again at this point.
[3] **L** adds 'and was buried' (not in **S, A, E, CH, TD**). The syntax suggests an interpolation.
[4] **S** has two leaves missing here; the lacuna can be filled from the Bohairic Coptic version.

And then, when he has come up, he shall be anointed from the oil[1] *of thanksgiving*[1] by the presbyter, who says:
    I anoint you with holy oil in the name of Jesus Christ.

And so each of them shall wipe themselves and put on their clothes, and then they shall enter into the church.

(Dix 22) And the bishop shall lay his hand on them and invoke, saying:
    Lord God, you have made them worthy to receive remission of sins through the laver of regeneration[2] of the holy Spirit:[2] send upon them your grace, that they may serve you according to your will; for to you is glory, to Father and Son with the holy Spirit in the holy Church, both now and to the ages of ages. Amen.

Then, pouring the oil of thanksgiving from his hand and placing it on his head, he shall say:
    I anoint you with holy oil in God the Father almighty and Christ Jesus and the holy Spirit.

And having signed him on the forehead, he shall give him a kiss and say:
    The Lord be with you.

And he who has been signed shall say:
    And with your spirit.

Come up] cf. Tertullian, *De Bapt.*, 7.
Oil of thanksgiving] i.e., oil which has been blessed.
Enter into the church] cf. chs.18, 35, 39, 41.
Lay his hand] cf. Tertullian, *De Bapt.*, 8.
The laver of regeneration] Titus 3.5. Dix regards **L** as corrupt at this point, and Botte suggests that a line has been left out in **L** or the Greek original. G. W. H. Lampe (Bibliography, 11) denies this, pointing out that **L** can be translated as it stands. In that case, the candidates have already received the holy Spirit in the water, and the bishop then prays for the sending of God's grace upon them; with the reading of Bohairic, **A,** and **E,** what they received in the water was forgiveness of sins, and the bishop now prays for them to be filled with the holy Spirit as the result of his laying-on of hands. The resemblance of the latter sequence of events to the later practice of Confirmation is obvious, and Dix actually inserted the title 'Confirmation' at this point. But he later wrote: 'I ought to have asked myself whether this was . . . the right place to make a break. [The original] makes no break from beginning to end' of the rite (*Theology of Confirmation*, p.12). (I owe this reference to Colin Buchanan).
Placing it on his head] Bohairic and **TD** read: 'placing his hand on his head'; **A** and **E** agree with **L**. Tertullian and the *Didascalia* support Bohairic and **TD**, but once again **L** makes sense as it stands.
A second post-baptismal anointing is unparalleled until the Gelasian Sacramentary.
Signed] Tertullian, *De Res. Carnis*, 8.
A kiss] **L**: *osculum;* not the kiss of peace, which is *'pacem'*, as below.

1-1 So Bohairic, **A, CH, TD; L:** 'which was sanctified'.
2-2 So **L;** Bohairic, **A, E** omit 'of the holy Spirit' and read 'make them worthy to be filled with the holy Spirit and'.

So let him do with each one. And then they shall pray together with all the people: they do not pray with the faithful until they have carried out all these things. And when they have prayed, they shall give the kiss of peace.

(Dix 23). And then the offering shall be presented by the deacons to the bishop; and he shall give thanks over the bread for the representation, which the Greeks call 'antitype', of the body of Christ; and over the cup mixed with wine for the antitype, which the Greeks call 'likeness', of the blood which was shed for all who have believed in him; and over milk and honey[1] mixed together in fulfilment of the promise which was made to the fathers, in which he said, 'a land flowing with milk and honey', in which also Christ gave his flesh, through which those who believe are nourished like little children, making the bitterness of the heart sweet by the gentleness of his word; and over water, as an offering to signify the washing, that the inner man also, which is the soul, may receive the same things as the body. And the bishop shall give a reason for all these things to those who receive.

And when he breaks the bread, in distributing fragments to each, he shall say:
    The bread of heaven in Christ Jesus.

And he who receives shall answer:
    Amen.

And if there are not enough presbyters, the deacons also shall hold the cups, and stand by in good order and reverence: first, he who holds the water; second, the milk; third, the wine. And they who receive shall taste of each[2] thrice, he who gives it saying:
    In God the Father almighty.

And he who receives shall say:
    Amen.

    And in the Lord Jesus Christ.
    (Amen).
    And in the holy Spirit and the holy Church.

And he shall say:
    Amen:
So shall it be done with each one.

Pray with the faithful] cf. Justin, *Apol.*, 65.1.
The kiss of peace] cf. Justin, *Apol.*, 65.2.
The offering] cf. Justin, *Apol,*, 65.3, and chapter 4, above.
The representation] cf. Tertullian, *Adv. Marc.*, 4.40: *id est figura corporis.*
The cup mixed] cf. Cyprian, *Letter 63*, passim.
'Likeness'] Botte (p.55 note 2) points out that the interpolations in **L** have confused the symmetry of the passage, and conjectures: 'the cup mixed with wine for the likeness, which the Greeks call *homoioma'.*
Milk and honey] cf. Tertullian, *De Corona*, 3.
Water] cf. Justin, *Apol.*, 65.3, 66.4.
Good order] **S** has *'eutaxia'* ='in the right order'. For deacons administering the chalice, cf. Cyprian, *De lapsis*, 25.

---

[1] **S** begins again here.
[2] Or '. . . taste of each, he who gives it saying thrice . . .'

When these things have been done, each one shall hasten to do good works
[1]*and to please God and to conduct himself rightly, being zealous for the
Church, doing what he has learnt and advancing in piety.*

*We have handed over to you in brief these things about holy baptism and
the holy offering, for you have already been instructed about the resurrection
of the flesh and the other things as it is written. But if there is anything
else which ought to be said, the bishop shall say it privately to those who
have received[2] baptism. Unbelievers must not get to know it, unless they
first receive[2] baptism. This is the white stone of which John said, 'A new
name is written on it, which no-one knows except him who receives the
stone'.*

(OF ADMINISTERING THE COMMUNION)[3]

22. *(Dix 24). On Saturday and Sunday the bishop himself, if possible,
shall distribute to all the people with his own hand; the deacons break, and
the presbyters shall break the bread. When a deacon takes it to a presbyter,
he shall hold out the paten,[4] and the presbyter himself shall take it and
distribute it to the people with his own hand. On other days they shall
receive as the bishop directs.*

OF FASTING[5]

23. *(Dix 25, 26.1a). Widows and virgins shall fast often and pray for the
Church. Presbyters shall fast if they wish, and laymen likewise. A bishop
cannot fast except when all the people do so. It happens that someone
wishes to make an offering, and he cannot refuse him; but in all cases he
breaks and tastes.*

Received] Botte regards the omission of 'baptism' in **A** and **E** as the better reading
(p.59 note 5). Instruction continued after first communion even in the
fourth century.

The white stone] Revelation 2.17.

22   This chapter follows 21 in **E** and, apparently, in **CH** and **TD**. In **CH** it applies to
communion for a sick priest, and ends: 'A deacon may distribute the offerings to the
people if the bishop or the priest allows it'. **TD** has a similar sentence.

Saturday] Probably added to conform with Ethiopian custom. *Pace* Dix and Botte,
there is some evidence for Christian worship on Saturdays in the 3rd century;
see C. W. Dugmore, *The Influence of the Synagogue upon the Divine Office,*
(S.P.C.K., London, 1968), pp.28-37.

The paten] This was the practice in the papal liturgy; see Dix, pp.82-3.

23   This chapter follows 22 in **E**, but in **S** and **A** it comes directly after 21.

An offering] For a meal, not for the eucharist.

---

[1] **L** breaks off again here.

[2] **A, E** omit 'baptism'; the passage might then refer to the eucharist.

[3] Title conjectural. This section is found in **E, CH, TD**; not in **L, S, A**.

[4] So **TD**; **E** reads 'his clothing'.

[5] This chapter is taken from the *Epitome,* which has the original Greek.

OF GIFTS TO THE SICK[1]

24. *(Dix 26.14-17). In an emergency a deacon shall give the sign to the sick with diligence, if no presbyter is present. And when he has given all that is needed for him to receive what is distributed, he shall give thanks, and they shall consume it there.*

THAT THOSE WHO HAVE RECEIVED SHOULD MINISTER DILIGENTLY[2]

If anyone has received anything to take to a widow, a sick person, or a church worker, he shall take it that day; and if he has not taken it, he shall take it the next day, adding to what there was from his own; because the bread of the poor remained with him.

OF THE BRINGING-IN OF LAMPS AT THE COMMUNAL SUPPER[3]

25. *(Dix 26.18-32). When the bishop is present, and evening has come, a deacon brings in a lamp; and standing in the midst of all the faithful who are present, (the bishop) shall give thanks. First he shall say this greeting:*

> *The Lord be with you.*

And the people shall say:

> *With your spirit.*
> *Let us give thanks to the Lord.*

And they shall say:

> *It is fitting and right: greatness and exaltation with glory are his due.*

And he does not say, 'Up with your hearts', because that is said (only) at the offering. And he shall pray thus, saying:

> *We give you thanks, Lord, through your Son Jesus Christ our Lord, through whom you have shone upon us and revealed to us the inextinguishable light. So when we have completed the length of the day and have come to the beginning of the night, and have satisfied ourselves with the light of day which you created for our satisfying; and since now through your grace we do not lack the light of evening, we praise and glorify you through your Son Jesus Christ our Lord, through whom be glory and power and honour to you with the holy Spirit, both now and always and to the ages of ages. Amen.*

---

24 This chapter follows 23 in **CH**, and 22 in **TD**, which omits 23. **E** has it after 29. but this is a less likely position since **L** goes straight from 29 to 30. Dix's note (p.83) is corrected by Chadwick (Dix-Chadwick, page *j*); cf. Botte, pp.xxxi, xxxii.

> The sign] **TD** interprets this as baptism; Dix suggests unction. The gloss in the next paragraph (note 2 below) may be an attempt to explain this unfamiliar term.

25 This chapter follows 24 in **E, CH,** and **TD;** and there would have been room for it in the pages missing from **L.** A slightly revised translation and discussion is to be found in Dix, *The Shape of the Liturgy,* pp.85ff.

> A lamp] cf. Tertullian, *Apol.,* 39: 'After water for the hands and lights . . .'

> Shall give thanks] Both **E** and **TD** appear to allot the initial greeting to the deacon; but there is a similar absence of subject in ch.5, where it can only be the bishop. Since there is no further change of subject here, and it must be the bishop who says the prayer (cf. **AC**), it is probable that 'the bishop' must be understood here.

---

[1] This chapter is found only in **E,** with hints in **CH** and **TD.** The text is confused.

[2] Botte conjectures that this sentence should be taken as a title. It is followed by an irrelevant gloss: 'He shall give the blessed bread'.

[3] This chapter is found only in **E,** with hints in **AC, CH,** and **TD.**

And all shall say:
        Amen.

They shall rise, then, after supper and pray; and the boys and the virgins shall say psalms.[1]

And then the deacon, when he receives the mixed cup of the offering, shall say a psalm from those in which 'Alleluia' is written, and then, if the priest so directs, again from the same psalms. And after the bishop has offered the cup, he shall say the whole of a psalm which applies to the cup, with 'Alleluia', all joining in. When they recite psalms, all shall say, 'Alleluia', which means, 'We praise him who is God; glory and praise to him who created every age through his word alone'. And when the psalm is finished, he shall give thanks over the cup and distribute the fragments to all the faithful.

OF THE COMMON MEAL[2]

26. *(Dix 26.1c-4). And when they have supper, the faithful who are present shall take from the bishop's hand a little bit of bread before they break their own bread; because it is blessed bread and not the eucharist, that is, the body of the Lord.*

OF THE TIME OF THE MEAL[3]

It is fitting that all, before they drink, should take a cup and give thanks over it, and so eat and drink in purity.

[4]. . . you who are present, and so feast. But to the catechumens shall be given exorcized bread, and each shall offer a cup.

They shall rise] 'Manifestly out of place' (Botte). The rest of this chapter is confused. Cf. Tertullian, *Apol.,* 39: 'Each is called into the midst to sing something from holy Scripture . . . Prayer ends the meal'.

If the priest so directs] Hanssens (II, 129) renders: 'The priest, if (the bishop) directs'.

The cup] Dix regards this as an error for 'bread'; but this is not a eucharist. Cf. *Didache* (9.1-3): 'Give thanks thus. First, about the cup . . . And about the broken bread . . .' 'Fragments' in the Ethiopic represents the Greek word *'klasmata',* also found in the *Didache*. Cf. also 1 Cor. 10.16.

26 This chapter follows 23 in **S** and **A**; **E** has it twice, once after 23 and again after 25: the latter is the version translated here. In **S** and **A** (and **E** the first time) this sentence has been prefixed to the chapter to cover the omission of 24 and 25: 'And when he breaks bread, he shall eat it' (Dix, 26.1b). A translation and discussion of this chapter will be found in Dix, *The Shape of the Liturgy*, pp.82-5.

You who are present] **L** reappears in the middle of a sentence whose construction is different from that of **S,** using the second person, as in ch.28.

---

[1] Hanssens: 'a psalm'.
[2] Chapter 26 is taken from **S.**
[3] This title is quite inappropriate, here or anywhere else.
[4] **L** resumes here.

THAT CATECHUMENS OUGHT NOT TO EAT WITH THE FAITHFUL

27. (Dix 26.5, 6). A catechumen shall not sit at the Lord's Supper. But through the whole meal he who *eats*[1] should remember him who invited him; because that is why he besought him to enter under his roof.

THAT ONE SHOULD EAT WITH TEMPERANCE AND MODERATION[2]

28. (Dix 26.7-12). When you eat and drink, do it discreetly and not to the point of drunkenness, and not so that anyone may laugh at you, or that he who invited you may be grieved by your disorderly behaviour, but so that he may pray to be made worthy that the saints may come in to him; for the Lord said, 'You are the salt of the earth'.

If an offering, which is called in Greek 'apophoreton', is made to all in common, accept some. If it is for all to eat, eat enough for there to be some over, which he who invited you may send to whom he wishes, as it were from the left-overs of the saints, and rejoice in confidence.

And let the guests, when they eat, receive in silence, not contending with words, but as the bishop allows; and if he has asked anything, an answer shall be given him. And when the bishop says a word, let all be modestly silent,[3] until he asks another question.

If the bishop is absent, but the faithful are at the supper in the presence of a priest or a deacon, let them eat in the same orderly way. And all shall hasten to receive the blessed bread from the hand of the priest or the deacon. Likewise a catechumen shall receive the same, exorcized. If the laity are together, they must behave in an orderly way, for a layman cannot make the blessed bread.

THAT ONE SHOULD EAT WITH THANKSGIVING

29. (Dix 26.13). Let everyone eat in the name of the Lord. For this is pleasing to God, that we should compete among the heathen in being like-minded and sober.

---

27 The faithful have received blessed bread and the catechumens exorcized bread; but the latter may not remain for the eucharist.
> He who eats] Dix later adopted this translation (*Shape*, p.82); the translator of **L** may have taken the verb as active ('offers') rather than middle ('helps himself').
> Invited] This is a private party, but a cleric must say grace (Dix, *Shape*, p.84).

28 When you eat] cf. Tertullian, *Apol.*, 39: 'What hungry men need is eaten, what befits prudent men is drunk'.
> For the Lord said] Matthew 5.13.
> Modestly silent] **L** adds *'laudans'*, possibly a copyist's error for *'audiens'*.

29 For this is pleasing] **S** reads: 'For this is fitting, that we should all be sober, that the heathen may envy us'.

---

[1] So **S, A, E; L:** 'offers' (cf. Dix, *The Shape of the Liturgy*, p.82).
[2] **A** adds 'and not get drunk'.
[3] **L** adds 'praising' (not in **S**).

HIPPOLYTUS: A TEXT FOR STUDENTS

OF SUPPER FOR WIDOWS

30. (Dix 27). If anyone wants widows to have a meal, let them be ripe in years, and let him send them away before the evening. And if he cannot (receive them) because of the charge which he has been allotted, let him give them food and wine, and send them away, and let them partake as they like at home.

OF THE FRUITS ONE SHOULD OFFER TO THE BISHOP[1]

31. (Dix 28.1-5). Let all hasten to offer the new fruits to the bishop as firstfruits. And *as he*[2] offers them, he shall bless them and name him who offered, saying:

> [3]We give you thanks, O God, and offer to you the firstfruits which you have granted us to receive; you nourished them by your word, and ordered the earth to bear all fruits for the joy and nourishment of men and for all animals. In all these things we praise you, O God, and in all the things with which you have helped us, adorning for us the whole creation with various fruits; through your child Jesus Christ our Lord, through whom be glory to you for the ages of ages. Amen.

OF THE BLESSING OF FRUITS[4]

32. (Dix 28.6-8). Fruits indeed are blessed, that is, grapes, figs, pomegranates, olives, pears, apples, mulberries, peaches, cherries, almonds, plums; but not pumpkins, melons, cucumbers, onions, garlic, or any other vegetable. But sometimes flowers also are offered.

[5]So let roses and lilies be offered, but not others. And in all things which are eaten, they shall give thanks to the holy God, eating to his glory.

THAT NO-ONE SHOULD TOUCH ANY FOOD AT THE PASCHA BEFORE THE PROPER TIME FOR EATING

33. (Dix 29). At the Pascha no-one may eat before the offering is made. If anyone does so, it does not count for him as fasting. Anyone who is pregnant or ill, and cannot fast for two days, should fast (only) on the Saturday on account of their necessity, confining themselves to bread and water. Anyone who was at sea or found himself in some necessity, and did not know the day, when he has learned of it, shall observe the fast after

---

30 At the end of this chapter **E** interpolates chapter 1 and a quantity of baptismal material (see Horner, pp.162-78).

31 **L** is confused, but its meaning is clear from **S**.

Name him who offered] **CH** and **TD** do so, unlike the other sources. **AC** explains that the fruits are for the nourishment of bishop, priests, and deacons; they are, in fact, tithes. Cf. Exod. 23.19 (LXX): 'You shall bring the first-fruits of the first crop into the house of the Lord your God'; *Didache,* 13.3: 'Take all firstfruits . . . and give them to the prophets'.

Your child] cf. chs. 3, 4, 7.

32 Melons . . . garlic] cf. Numbers 11.5, which has 'leeks' instead of 'pumpkins'; **S** has both. Cf. *Mishnah, Tr. Maaseroth,* 1.2, 3 (ed. Danby, p.66).

---

[1] This title and that of chapter 32 seem to have got transposed.

[2] **L**: 'and he who offers' (probably misunderstanding the Greek).

[3] The prayer is found in the *Barberini Euchologion* (*c.*800) in a faulty Greek text (Botte, p.76; Dix, p.54) which nevertheless largely confirms **L**.

[4] See note 1 above.

[5] **L** has a space here for a title.

Pentecost. For the type has passed away: that is why it ended in the second month; and when he has learned the truth, he should observe the fast.

THAT DEACONS SHOULD ATTEND ON THE BISHOP
34. (Dix 30). Each deacon, with the subdeacons, shall attend on the bishop. They shall inform him of those who are ill, so that, if he pleases, he may visit them. For a sick man is greatly comforted when the high-priest remembers him.

OF THE TIME WHEN ONE OUGHT TO PRAY[1]
35. (Dix 31). The faithful, as soon as they have woken and got up, before they turn to their work, shall pray to God, and so hasten to their work. If there is any verbal instruction, one should give preference to this, and go to hear the word of God, to the comfort of his soul. Let him hasten to the church, where the Spirit flourishes.

THAT THE EUCHARIST SHOULD BE RECEIVED FIRST, WHENEVER IT IS OFFERED, BEFORE ANY FOOD IS TAKEN[2]
36. (Dix 32.1). Let every one of the faithful take steps to receive the eucharist before he eats anything else. For if he receives in faith, even if some deadly thing is given him, after that it shall not overpower him.

THAT THE EUCHARIST MUST BE CAREFULLY GUARDED
37. (Dix 32.2). Let everyone take care that no unbeliever eats of the eucharist, nor any mouse or other animal, and that none of it falls and is lost. For it is the body of Christ, to be eaten by believers, and not to be despised.

---

33   The type] i.e., the Jewish Passover, which is over after seven weeks. The versions are confused, and the exact meaning of the last sentence remains obscure, though Botte goes some way towards making sense of it (p.81 notes 2 and 3).

35   It appears from **L** that there were two forms of **AT** in circulation, which had different endings and were later combined. One form went straight from the end of 38 to 42 and 43, the other had 38-43 complete, with a slightly different version of 42 and 43. The shorter version is printed in the text after 38 as 42A and 43A, the longer after 41 as 42B and 43B. 42A and 43A are peculiar to **L,** and do not appear in any other source. Although the longer ending includes an expanded version of 35 as 41, 35 was still kept when the two forms were combined.

39-41 are found in **S, A, E,** and **CH,** 40 also in **TD,** 41 also in **TD** and **AC,** so there can be no doubt of their authenticity.

In the church] cf. chs.18, 21, 39, 41.

36   **TD** places this chapter after 41. Dix (p.xlv note †) quotes Jerome as apparently referring to this passage.

Overpower him] Mark 16.18; **L** has 'harm him', which is closer to the NT text.

37   As Dix points out (p.84), this chapter and the next refer to communion from the reserved sacrament at home. The communicant himself 'blesses a cup'. cf. the liturgy of the Pre-Sanctified, 'a purely *local* Roman custom'; also Cyprian, *De lapsis*, 26, for reservation at home. Dix offers a revised translation of chs. 36-38 in his *A Detection of Aumbries* (1941), pp.6-7.

---

[1] Another version of chapter 35 appears below as chapter 41.

[2] The original Greek text of this chapter has been preserved in two MSS, one of which is known as the 'Ochrid fragment' (Botte, p.82; Dix-Chadwick, p. *c*).

NOTHING MUST FALL FROM THE CUP

38. (Dix 32.3, 4). For having blessed (the cup) in the name of God, you received as it were the antitype of the blood of Christ. Therefore do not pour any out, as though you despised it, lest an alien spirit lick it up. You will be guilty of the blood, as one who despises the price with which he has been bought.

OF THE SIGN OF THE CROSS[1]

42A. (Dix 37a). [2]*If you are tempted,* sign your forehead. For this sign of the passion is displayed against the Devil, if it is made in faith, not to please men, but through knowledge, presenting it like a breastplate. For when the Adversary sees the power of the Spirit (which comes) from the heart, outwardly displayed in the likeness of baptism, he will tremble and flee, when you do not strike him but breathe on him. Moses did this symbolically with the sheep which was sacrificed at the Passover. By sprinkling the blood on the threshold and by anointing the two doorposts, he signified that faith which is now in us, in the perfect sheep. Let us sign forehead and eyes with the hand, and escape from him who is trying to destroy us.

43A. (Dix 38.1, 2). And so, when these things are heard with thankfulness and true [3]orthodox faith, they provide edification for the Church and eternal life for believers. I counsel those who are sensible to guard them. For to all who hear the apos(tolic tradition) . . .[4]

39. *(Dix 33).* [5]*The deacons and priests shall assemble daily at the place which the bishop appoints for them. Let the deacons not fail to assemble at all times, unless illness hinders them. When all have assembled, let them teach those who are in the church, and in this way, when they have prayed, let each one go to the work which falls to him.*

OF CEMETERIES[6]

40. *(Dix 34). No man may be heavily charged for burying a man in the cemeteries; it is the property of all the poor. But the fee of the workman*

---

38 Antitype] cf. ch.21.   Alien] cf. chs.20, 21, 42A.

42A If you are tempted] cf. Tertullian, *De Corona,* 3.

    Strike] **L:** *caedente* =Greek *'tuptontos'* changed in 42B to *'ptuontos',* i.e., 'spitting'.

    Sprinkling] Exodus 12.7; Dix, pp.85-6 (but the sermons quoted are not now attributed to Hippolytus; see note on ch.4).

39 This chapter follows 38 in **S** without any title; in **A** and **E** it has a fresh number, and a title made by repeating the first sentence.

    In the church] cf. chs.18, 21, 35, 41.

40 Dix (p.xxxvi) points out that Hippolytus' enemy Callistus was the first administrator of the earliest Christian cemetery.

---

[1] Another version of this chapter appears below as chapter 42B.

[2] Botte conjectures that *ei peirastho* ('if you are tempted') has been misread as *aei peirastho* ('always try'); so **L.**

[3] **L:** *recta gloriosae,* mistranslating the Greek word *orthodoxes.*

[4] **L** breaks off again here.

[5] This paragraph is taken from **S,** where it has no title.

[6] This chapter and the next are taken from **S.**

and the price of the tiles shall be paid to him who digs. The bishop shall provide for those who are in that place and look after it, so that there may be no heavy charge for those who come to those places.

OF THE TIME WHEN ONE OUGHT TO PRAY[1]

41. *(Dix 35, 36). Let every faithful man and woman, when they have risen from sleep in the morning, before they touch any work at all, wash their hands and pray to God, and so go to their work. But if instruction [2]in the word of God is given, each one should choose to go to that place, reckoning in his heart that it is God whom he hears in the instructor.*

For he who prays in the church will be able to pass by the wickedness of the day. He who is pious should think it a great evil if he does not go to the place where instruction is given, and especially if he can read, or if a teacher comes. Let none of you be late in the church, the place where teaching is given. Then it shall be given to the speaker to say that is useful to each one; you will hear things which you do not think of, and profit from things which the holy Spirit will give you through the instructor. In this way your faith will be strengthened about the things you will have heard. You will also be told in that place what you ought to do at home. Therefore let each one be diligent in coming to the church, the place where the holy Spirit flourishes. (Dix 36) If there is a day when there is no instruction, let each one, when he is at home, take up a holy book and read in it sufficiently what seems to him to bring profit.

And if you are at home, pray at the third hour and bless God. But if you are somewhere else at that moment, pray to God in your heart. For at that hour Christ was nailed to the tree. For this reason also in the Old (Testament) the Law prescribed that the shewbread should be offered [3]continually as a type of the body and blood of Christ; and the slaughter of the lamb without reason is this type of the perfect lamb. For Christ is the shepherd, and also the bread which came down from heaven.

The bishop shall provide] **A** and **E** add: 'from what is given to the churches'.

41   The seven hours of prayer (on waking, the third hour, the sixth hour, the ninth hour, before going to bed, about midnight, about cockcrow), though here appointed as times for private prayer, are obviously the prototypes of the monastic hours. The third and ninth hours and the lighting of lamps are probably derived from Jewish practice. Cf. also Tertullian: third, sixth, and ninth hours, *De Orat.,* 25; morning and evening, *ibid.,* 42; midnight, *Ad uxorem,* 2.4.

Wash] Standard Rabbinic practice before prayer.

In the church] cf. chs.18, 21, 35, 39.

The third, sixth, ninth hour] Mark 16.25, 33, 34; Tertullian, *De Orat.,* 25.

The shewbread] Dix and Botte prefer the reading of **A** and **E**; but the shewbread is not related to any particular hour. Rather, the stress is on its permanence, cf. 2 Chron. 2.4. **A** and **E** have been misled by the context.

The shepherd . . . heaven] John 10.14, 6.51.

---

[1] This chapter is taken from **S.**

[2] So *Epitome,* reproducing **AC; S:** 'instruction and the word . . .'

[3] **S:** 'every hour'; **A, E:** 'at the third hour'.

Pray likewise at the time of the sixth hour. For when Christ was nailed to the wood of the cross, the day was divided, and darkness fell. And so at that hour let them pray a powerful prayer, imitating the voice of him who prayed and made all creation dark for the unbelieving Jews.

And at the ninth hour let them pray also a great prayer and a great blessing, to know the way in which the soul of the righteous blesses

[1]God who does not lie, who remembered his saints and sent his word to give them light. For at that hour Christ was pierced in his side and poured out water and blood; giving light to the rest of the time of the day, he brought it to evening. Then, in beginning to sleep and making the beginning of another day, he fulfilled the type of the resurrection.

Pray before your body rests on the bed. Rise about midnight, wash your hands with water, and pray. If your wife is present also, pray both together; if she is not yet among the faithful, go apart into another room and pray, and go back to bed again. Do not be lazy about praying. He who is bound in the marriage-bond is not defiled.

Those who have washed have no need to wash again, for they are clean. By signing yourself with moist breath and catching your spittle in your hand, your body is sanctified down to your feet. For when (prayer) is offered with a believing heart as though from the font, the gift of the Spirit and the sprinkling of baptism sanctify him who believes. Therefore it is necessary to pray at this hour.

For the elders who gave us the tradition taught us that at that hour all creation is still for a moment, to praise the Lord; stars, trees, waters stop for an instant, and all the host of angels (which) ministers to him praises God with the souls of the righteous in this hour. That is why believers should take good care to pray at this hour.

Bearing witness to this, the Lord says thus, 'Lo, about midnight a shout was made of men saying, Lo, the bridegroom comes; rise to meet him'. And he goes on, saying, 'Watch therefore, for you know not at what hour he comes.'

To know] **S** reads *'eime'* ('know'); Botte conjectures *'eine'* ('be like').

Christ was pierced] As Botte points out, the reference is not to John 19.34, which has 'blood' before 'water', but to Matthew 27.49 (reading of Sinaiticus, Vaticanus, etc.), which places the piercing before Christ's death, as here, and 'water' before 'blood'.

Do not be lazy . . . defiled] **S**: 'Do not hesitate to pray, you who are bound in the marriage-bond, for you are not defiled'. The Rabbis forbade prayer and the study of the Torah after sexual intercourse.

Those who have washed] John 13.10.

Spittle] **L** has *'spm'*, which might be an abbreviation of either *'sputum'* or *'spiritum'*. **S, A, E** have 'spittle', and since the Greek words cannot be confused with one another, this is probably right.

All creation is still] cf. Vergil, *Aeneid,* IV. 522-7.

The host of angels] The construction requires the addition of 'which'.

The Lord says] Matthew 25.6, 13.

---

[1] **L** resumes here.

And likewise rise about cockcrow, [1]*and pray.* For at that hour, as the cock crew, the children of Israel denied Christ, whom we know by faith, our eyes looking towards that day in the hope of eternal light at the resurrection of the dead.

And if you act so, all you faithful, and remember these things, and teach them in your turn, and encourage the catechumens, you will not be able to be tempted or to perish since you have Christ always in memory.

42B. (Dix 37). Always reverently observe to sign your forehead. For this sign of the passion is known and approved against the devil, if you make it in faith, and not so that you may be seen by men, but through knowledge presenting it like a shield. For when the Adversary sees the power which comes from the heart, [2]*and when he sees the inner rational man, signed within and without with the sign of the word of God, he flees at once, expelled by the holy Spirit, who is in (every) man who makes a place for him in himself.*[2] Moses did this symbolically with the sheep which was sacrificed at the Passover; by sprinkling the blood on the threshold and anointing the doorposts, he signified that faith which is now in us, in the perfect sheep. So let us sign forehead and eyes with the hand, and escape from him who is trying to destroy us.

43B. (Dix 38b). And so if these things are received with thankfulness and true faith, they provide edification in the Church and eternal life for believers. I counsel that these things should be guarded by all those who are sensible. For if all of you hear the apostolic tra(dition),
                                    [3]*and follow it and keep it, no heretic or any man at all can lead you into error. For in this way many heresies have grown, because the leaders were not willing to learn the purpose of the apostles, but did what they wanted, according to their own pleasure, and not what was fitting.*

If we have passed over anything, beloved, God will reveal it to those who are worthy, since he steers the Church [4]*to the haven of quietness.*

42B See the note on ch.35. There is no title or new chapter here in any of the sources.
　　　A man displays] See the reading of **L** in the footnote. Botte suggests that a line has fallen out, so that the passage may have read: 'as the inner man, who is rational, displays the inner likeness of the word outwardly formed'.
　　　Spitting (note 2 below)] See the note on ch.42A.
　　　Sprinkling] See the note on ch.42A.
43 　Worthy (note 4 below)] Dix suggests that **S** read *'axian'* for *'hagian'* (p.72).

---

[1] So **S, A, E; L** omits.

[2] The rest of this sentence is taken from **S. L** is very confused, reading: 'as a man displays the outwardly formed image of the word, is routed, not by your spitting, but by your breathing with your mouth'.

[3] **L** breaks off again; the last few lines are taken from **S**.

[4] So **E; S**: 'the Church, which is worthy, to reach the haven of quietness'.

Books and articles in English

[*JTS=Journal of Theological Studies; SP=Studia Patristica*]

1. L. Bouyer, *Eucharist* (Notre Dame, 1970) pp.158-82.
2. R. H. Connolly, *The so-called Egyptian Church Order and derived documents* (Cambridge, 1916).
3. — 'The prologue to the *Apostolic Tradition* of Hippolytus' in *JTS* 22 (1921) pp.356-61.
4. — 'On the text of the baptismal creed of Hippolytus' in *JTS* 25 (1924), pp.131-9.
5. — 'The eucharistic prayer of Hippolytus' in *JTS* 39 (1938), pp.350-69.
5a. J. H. Crehan *Early Christian Baptism and the Creed* (London, 1950), Appendix IV, 'The Text of Hippolytus', pp.159-170.
6. G. Dix, *The Shape of the Liturgy* (Dacre/Black, London, 1945), pp.82-5, 157-62.
7. — 'The Ministry in the Early Church', in K. E. Kirk (ed.), *The Apostolic Ministry* (London, 1946) pp.192-201, 213-27.
8. W. H. Frere, 'Early Ordination Services' in *JTS* 16 (1915) pp.323-71.
9. D. L. Holland, 'The baptismal interrogation concerning the Holy Spirit in Hippolytus' in *SP* 10 (1970) pp.360-5.
10. J. A. Jungmann, *The Early Liturgy* (D.L.T., London, 1960) pp.52-86, 101-8.
11. G. W. H. Lampe, *The Seal of the Spirit* (Longmans, London, 1951) pp.128-42.
12. E. C. Ratcliff, 'The Sanctus and the pattern of the early Anaphora' in *Journal of Ecclesiastical History* 1 (1950) pp.29-36, 125-34. Reprinted in A. H. Couratin and D. Tripp (Ed.) *E. C. Ratcliff: Liturgical Studies* (S.P.C.K., London, 1976) pp.18-40.
13. — *'Apostolic Tradition:* questions concerning the appointment of the Bishop' in *SP* 8 (1966) pp.266-70. Reprinted as above, pp.156-60.
14. C. C. Richardson, 'The so-called epiclesis in Hippolytus' in *Harvard Theological Review* 40 (1947) pp.101-8.
15. — 'A note on the epicleses in Hippolytus and the Testamentum Domini' in *Recherches de théologie ancienne et mediévale* 15 (1948) pp.357-9.
16. — 'The date and setting of the Apostolic Tradition of Hippolytus' in *Anglican Theological Review* (USA) 30 (1948) pp.38-44.
17. E. Segelberg, 'The Ordination Prayers in Hippolytus' in *SP* 13 (1975) pp.397-408.
18. M. A. Smith, 'The anaphora of *Apostolic Tradition* re-considered' in *SP* 10 (1970) pp.426-30.
19. A. F. Walls, 'A note on the apostolic claim in the Church Order literature' in *SP* 2 (1957) pp.83-92.
20. — 'The Latin version of Hippolytus' *Apostolic Tradition'* in *SP* 3 (1961) pp.155-62.
21. R. J. Z. Werblowsky, 'On the baptismal rite according to St. Hippolytus' in *SP* 2 (1957), pp.93-105.

For **books and articles in French and German,** see Dix-Chadwick, pages *n, o, p.* To these should be added:

22. B. Botte, 'A propos de la Tradition apostolique' in *Recherches de théologie ancienne et mediévale* 33 (1966), pp.177-86.
23. —'Les plus anciennes collections canoniques' in *L'Orient Syrien* 5 (1960) pp.331-49.
24. — 'Tradition apostolique et Canon romain' in *La Maison-Dieu* 87 (1966) pp.52-61.